No. ______

In the Supreme Court of the United States

♦

Sam Sloan,
Richard Bozulich,
Thomas R. Stevens,
Petitioners,
-against-

Daniel S. Szalkiewicz,
Salvatore G. Caruso,
Board of Elections in the City of New York,
Attorney General of the State of New York

♦

On Petition for a Writ of Certiorari to the New York State Supreme Court, Appellate Division, First Department

♦

PETITION FOR A WRIT OF CERTIORARI

♦

Samuel H. Sloan
1664 Davidson Ave., Apt. 1B
Bronx NY 10453

917-507-7226
917-659-3397
samhsloan@gmail.com

Questions Presented

Where the Board of Elections in the City of New York has a rule under which any candidate for election in a recognized political party who wishes to be placed on the ballot must collect a sufficient of number of signatures from members of that party and those signatures must also be witnessed by a "subscribing witness" who must also be an enrolled member of that political party, does this rule constitute an unconstitutional infringement of the First and Fourteenth Amendment Constitutional Rights "to petition the Government" as well as an unconstitutional infringement on the right to vote and the right to Freedom of Association?

Where, as here, a sufficient number of signatures were collected from Republican Party Members which resulted in these candidates being placed on the ballot as Republican Party Candidates, but the candidates were removed from the ballot solely because the vast majority of the signatures were not witnessed by enrolled members of the Republican Party but instead were witnessed by other enrolled voters including Blanks, Democrats and Libertarians, should this court order that these three petitioner-candidates be reinstated on the ballot?

Table of Contents

Petition for a Writ of Certiorari

Petitioner Respectfully Prays that a Writ of Certiorari issue to the Supreme Court of the State of New York, Appellate Division, First Department to review the decision of the Supreme Court of the State of New York dated August 9, 2013, Index No. 101087/2013, and the decision of the Appellate Division, First Department of the Supreme Court of the State of New York dated August 13, 2013 which denied the validation petition of the above candidates to be reinstated on the ballot after these candidates were removed from the ballot solely because their petition signatures had not been witnessed by enrolled Republicans.

On August 21, 2013, the Court of Appeals of the State of New York denied the motion by Petitioner for Leave to Appeal to the New York Court of Appeals.

Parties to the Case

Daniel S. Szalkiewicz
Attorney for Self and Salvatore Caruso
280 Riverside Drive
New York NY 10025

Stephen Kitzinger
New York City Law Department
100 Church Street
New York NY 10007

Stephen H. Richman
Board of Elections in the City of New York
32 Broadway, 7th Floor
New York NY 10004

Richard P. Dearing
Deputy Solicitor General
Attorney General of New York
120 Broadway
New York NY 10005
212-416-6685

Constitutional Provisions Involved

The First Amendment to the United States Constitution provides:

"Congress shall make no law respecting an establishment of religion, or prohibiting the free exercise thereof; or abridging the freedom of speech, or of the press; or the right of the people peaceably to assemble, and to petition the government for a redress of grievances."

Section One of the Fourteenth Amendment to the United States Constitution provides:

[N]or shall any State deprive any person of life, liberty, or property, without due process of law . . . .

The statute which under the interpretation by the Board of Elections requires the mere witnesses to be Republicans is Section 132 (2) of New York Election law which states:

> There shall be appended at the bottom of each sheet a signed

statement of a witness who is a duly qualified voter of the state and an enrolled voter of the same political party as the voters qualified to sign the petition, and who is also a resident of the political subdivision in which the office or position is to be voted for.

Table of Cases

Credico v. New York State Bd. of Elections, 751 F.Supp.2d 417, 423 (E.D.N.Y. 2010)

Dekom vs. New York, 12-CV-1318 (JS)(ARL)

Kaloshi v. Hackshaw, 02 CV 4762, 2002 WL 31051530 (E.D.N.Y. Sept. 6, 2002)

Lerman v. Bd. of Elections of N.Y.C., 232 F.3d 135, 145 (2d Cir. 2000).

Maslow v. Board of Elections in City of N.Y., 658 F.3d 291 (2d Cir. 2011)

Yick Wo Vs. Hopkins, 118 US 356, 370 (1886)

N.Y. State Bd. of Elections v. Lopez-Torres, 552 U.S. 196, 128 S.Ct. 791, 798, 169 L.Ed.2d 665 (2008)

OPINIONS BELOW

There are no opinions below. Neither the New York Supreme Court, nor the Appellate Division of the

Supreme Court First Department nor the New York Court of Appeals issued an opinion on this case.

Jurisdiction

The Candidate-Petitioners and their supporters circulated petitions to be placed on the ballot. Petitions containing more than 4500 signatures were timely filed by "Cindarella Time" which was midnight on July 11, 2013. As this filing was facially valid, petitioner-candidates were placed on the ballot. However, a General Objection by one Sal Caruso was filed on July 15, 2013 followed by a Specific Objection on July 22, 2013. A hearing was held before the New York Board of Elections on July 30, 2013 following which these candidates were kicked off the ballot on July 31, 2013 for one reason only which was 3905 of these signatures had not been witnessed by enrolled members of the Republican Party. Rather the signatures had been witnessed by other voters including Democrats, Libertarians and Blanks.

Petitioners filed a petition to validate their places on the ballot on August 1, 2013. A show cause order was issued requiring the objector and the Board of Elections to appear on August 5, 2013. On August 9, 2013 Judge Wooten denied the Validation Petition without opinion. Petitioner appealed and this appeal was heard by the New York Supreme Court Appellate Division First Department which affirmed the decision of the Supreme Court without opinion. Petitioner then filed a motion for leave to appeal with the Court of Appeals of New York. This was denied on August 21, 2013. This petition for Certiorari follows.

Statement of the Case

This proceeding is brought under Election Law Sections 16-100 and 16-102 and other provisions of New York Law. Sam Sloan is a candidate for Mayor of the City of New York. Richard Bozulich is a candidate for Comptroller of the City of New York. Thomas R. Stevens is a candidate for Public Advocate of the City of New York.

Supporters of the candidates circulated petitions and the requisite number of signatures were obtained to get on the ballot. The signed petitions were timely submitted to the Board of Elections in the City of New York. The Petitions complied in every respect with the election rules, including cover sheets and wording of the petitions. There were enough signatures, the cover sheet was done properly and the wording of the petition was correct.

However, on July 31, 2013, all three of these candidates were thrown off the ballot after a hearing by the New York City Board of Elections for one reason only, which was that these were designating petitions for the Republican Party Primary, and the subscribing witnesses (not the signers) were not registered as Republicans with the New York City Board of Elections.

Unfortunately, the candidates had not been previously aware that there was any rule requiring that the mere witnesses to a petition be members of any political party. Had they known about this rule they might have been able to take appropriate action on time (although this would have been difficult as there are few Republicans willing to perform this task of witnessing signatures which may expose them to civil liability).

The statute which under the interpretation by the Board of Elections requires the mere witnesses to be Republicans is Section 132 (2) of New York Election law which states:

> There shall be appended at the bottom of each sheet a signed statement of a witness who is a duly qualified voter of the state and an enrolled voter of the same political party as the voters qualified to sign the petition, and who is also a resident of the political subdivision in which the office or position is to be voted for.

This provision was declared unconstitutional in the case Lerman v. Bd. of Elections of N.Y.C., 232 F.3d 135, 145 (2d Cir. 2000). This is explained in Dekom vs. New York, 12-CV-1318 (JS)(ARL).

However, at the hearing of this appeal before the Appellate Division on August 13, 2013, counsel for the Board of Elections and the Department of Law suggested that the Lerner decision has been overruled by the Maslow case, which is Maslow v. Board of Elections in City of N.Y., 658 F.3d 291 (2d Cir. 2011).

Petitioner-Appellant contends that the Maslow case has nothing to do with the instant case because the

Maslow Case was a test case for declaratory relief, not an actual case, whereas in the instant the petitioners have been trying hard to get on the ballot and have spent considerable money to do so, yet have been thwarted by an unwritten rule they had no way to know about.

The First Amendment to the Constitution provides:

> "Congress shall make no law respecting an establishment of religion, or prohibiting the free exercise thereof; or abridging the freedom of speech, or of the press; or the right of the people peaceably to assemble, and to petition the government for a redress of grievances."

Here the law clearly infringes the Constitutional Right "to petition the government". There have been several cases on this subject, but all of them have been federal cases. Petitioner maintains that the state courts are just as competent and capable to decide constitutional issues as the federal courts are.

The subscribing witness rule was found unconstitutional in Kaloshi v. New York City Board of Elections, 02 CV 4762, 2002 WL 31051530 (E.D.N.Y. Sept. 6, 2002). This is a lengthy and reasoned opinion that declared the specific statute in question to be unconstitutional. This is the only reported case that deals directly with this statute.

It appears from the oral argument held before the Appellate Division and the Court of Appeals that counsel for the Board of Elections would also like to see this case reviewed by this court because he believes the Lerner Decision was effectively overruled by the Maslow decision. The Lerner decision has been a thorn in the side for the Board of Elections as the Board of Elections has difficulty checking voter registrations in upstate New York and this constantly causes problems in New York City Elections.

The main operative fact is it is undisputed that the petitioners collected 3905 valid signatures whereas only 3750 are required, except that these 3905 signatures were declared invalid because the signatures were not witnessed by Republicans. While there have been several federal cases related to this issue, there has never been a reported state case on this issue, and thus this motion for leave to appeal should be granted.

Reasons for Granting the Writ

It is difficult to imagine a more obvious constitutional right than the Right to Petition the Government. Requiring that petitions be witnessed by Republicans and by nobody else is such an obvious infringement that it is difficult to imagine that anybody could defend it.

This requirement has been struck down in two federal cases, namely Kaloshi v. New York City Board of Elections, 02 CV 4762, 2002 WL 31051530 (E.D.N.Y. Sept. 6, 2002) and Lerman v. Bd. of Elections of N.Y.C., 232 F.3d 135, 145 (2d Cir. 2000).

However, the Board of Elections claims that those two decisions are no longer good law and were overruled by Maslow v. Board of Elections in City of N.Y., 658 F.3d 291 (2d Cir. 2011) and N.Y. State Bd. of Elections v. Lopez-Torres, 552 U.S. 196, 128 S.Ct. 791, 798, 169 L.Ed.2d 665 (2008).

Petitioner disagrees. With an election coming up, certiorari should be granted to decide these important questions.

This document is prepared in Century Schoolbook New Bold 12 point with a word count of 2172 words.

Dated August 23, 2013 Respectfully Submitted,

Samuel H. Sloan
1664 Davidson Ave Apt 1B
Bronx NY 10453
917-507-7226
917-659-3397
samhsloan@gmail.com

Appendix A

Transcript of Hearing Before Judge Paul Wooten

1

SUPREME COURT OF THE STATE OF NEW YORK
COUNTY OF NEW YORK: CIVIL TERM: PART 7
--X
SAMUEL H. SLOAN, RICHARD BOZULICH, THOMAS R.
STEVENS,

Petitioners
Index No:
-against- 101087/2013

DANIEL S. SZALKIEWICZ, SALVATORE G. CARUSO,
BOARD OF ELECTIONS IN THE CITY OF NEW YORK,

Respondents.
--X
60 Centre Street
New York, New York 10007
August 5, 2013
B E F O R E:
THE HONORABLE PAUL WOOTEN,
J U S T I C E
A P P E A R A N C E S:

SAMUEL H. SLOAN
Petitioner Pro Se
1664 Davidson Avenue, Apt. 1B
Bronx NY 10453

DANIEL S. SZALKIEWICZ, ESQ.
Attorney for Respondent Salvatore Caruso
280 Riverside Drive
New York, NY 10025

NEW YORK CITY LAW DEPARTMENT OFFICE OF THE CORPORATION COUNSEL
100 Church Street
New York, NY 10007
BY: Stephen Kitzinger, Esq.

BOARD OF ELECTIONS CITY OF NEW YORK
32 Broadway - 7th Floor
New York, NY 10004
BY: Steven H. Richman, Esq.

VANESSA MILLER
Senior Court Reporter

2

Proceedings

THE COURT: Calling the case of Sloan versus Szalkiewicz, index number 101087 of 2013.

Who represents Mr. Sloan?

MR. SLOAN: That's me. I'm representing myself.

THE COURT: And who represents Mr. Szalkiewicz?

MR. SZALKIEWICZ: Your Honor, I am Mr. Szalkiewicz and I represent Salvadore G. Caruso who's actually the objector. I'm not sure why I'm personally named.

THE COURT: You are.

MR. SZALKIEWICZ: I was his counsel at the time and I guess my name was on the spec as a contact individual.

THE COURT: Okay.

MR. SZALKIEWICZ: But I am Mr. Caruso's attorney as well.

THE COURT: Okay. Very well.

Any objection to Mr. Szalkiewicz representing Mr. Caruso from any of the parties?

MR. SLOAN: I have no objection to that, your Honor. But one thing I do object to is it's obvious that Mr. Caruso is a front man and I would like to know who's paying Mr. Szalkiewicz's legal fees because he's obviously got some others behind him who are doing this.

THE COURT: That's a request by you, sir?

MR. SLOAN: Yes, it is.

THE COURT: Your application is denied. We've never done that. In 30 years on the bench we've never, never -- I'm sorry. In five years on the bench and 27 years as an election law attorney, we've never had a case where that application's been granted. You have an exception, sir.

Who represents the Board?

MR. KITZINGER: Stephen Kitzinger, New York City Law Department.

MR. RICHMAN: Steven Richman, counsel for the respondent, Board of Elections.

THE COURT: Okay. Let the record reflect that I'm joined by Mr. Jack Suiter (ph), one of our principal law clerks who assists in this special election part.

All right. So was there a Board report here, sir?

MR. KITZINGER: Your Honor, there was a Board report. But, initially, I believe there are three named plaintiffs and two of them are not present.

THE COURT: Okay.

MR. KITZINGER: So I think their claims should

be dismissed.

THE COURT: Is Mr. Stevens here?

4

Proceedings

MR. SLOAN: No, he's not here.

THE COURT: Okay. Is Mr. Richard – how do you –

MR. SLOAN: Bozulich. He's out of the country.

THE COURT: Okay. So two of the petitioners are not represented here today?

MR. SLOAN: That's correct, your Honor.

THE COURT: Okay. So do they plan to be represented? Do they have an attorney?

MR. SLOAN: I just don't know.

THE COURT: Okay. So you don't know if they're planning to be represented. I can't take your word that one of them is out of the country. I do know that the two are not here. It is now, approximately, 10:35. I will give them to 11:00 a.m. where I'll second-call the case to see if they appear.

But on your application, Mr. Sloan, which is an application for an order to validate to put you on the ballot for the Office Of Mayor of the City of New York on the Republican party for the September primary; is that correct?

MR. SLOAN: Yes, your Honor.

THE COURT: Very well. Have you served your affidavit of service?

MR. SLOAN: Yes, I have.

THE COURT: Do you have them?

MR. SLOAN: Yes, I do.

MR. KITZINGER: I have it too --

THE COURT: Just a moment. Let's go through procedure. Mr. Sloan.

(Handing.)

THE COURT: Okay. Officer Burgos, would you show the affidavit of service to the respondents please?

(Handing.)

MR. KITZINGER: I don't see an affidavit of service on the Board.

MR. SLOAN: Oh. They time-stamped it. It's in the back. I have to search for it. They have a time stamp from the Board of Elections.

THE COURT: One of them is time-stamped; isn't it?

MR. KITZINGER: Actually, I see time-stamped copies, I mean, if the Court is going to accept that.

THE COURT: Okay. At this particular time, I'm showing you the affidavit of service.

(Handing.)

THE COURT: Are there any objections to in personam jurisdiction?

MR. KITZINGER: None from the Board, your Honor.

THE COURT: Okay.

MR. SZALKIEWICZ: I mean, if I may, the only

way I would object is depending on who actually served it on the Board, I'm not sure what individual did it. If it was Mr. Sloan, I would object to it in that he's actually a candidate and under CPLR 2103, he's unable to serve the Board personally. As we don't have an affidavit of service on behalf of the Board, I'd object until we can learn actually who is the actual individual that did it.

(Pause in proceedings.)

MR. SZALKIEWICZ: Your Honor, if I may also, it's --

THE COURT: Anything additional?

MR. SZALKIEWICZ: Yes, it's my understanding and basis upon information and belief that correspondence that was sent by Mr. Sloan himself, that he was additionally present. He says he himself that he left the court papers with the doorman at my office address. If he was the individual that was either with him or left them himself, then I would be contesting the affidavit of service. And I also believe it violates the spirit of the law that the party himself was present and apparently questioned certain individuals at the time of service.

THE COURT: Well, what we have here is we have

an affidavit of service by Mr. George Rankoth who said

that he served this on August 21st at 7:45 –

MR. SLOAN: August 1st.

THE COURT: August 1st, 2013 at 7:45 a.m. –

MR. SLOAN: It should say p.m.

THE COURT: All right. It's not circled, but you're telling me it's meant to be 7:45 p.m.

And then there's a second affidavit of service that says 10:45 p.m., which is the petition. The mere fact that there's an allegation that one of the parties was present with the process server doesn't invalidate the service.

MR. SZALKIEWICZ: I'll waive the objection then.

THE COURT: Okay. That's number one.

So your objection to in personam jurisdiction on the basis of him being present then is inappropriate. The question is an affidavit of service creates a presumption which you have to rebut at the particular time, that's insufficient to rebut the presumption.

The question here is on the Board of Election cases, there is a Board of Election time stamp. In the past, we have created that the Board of Election time stamp is the same as an affidavit which creates a presumption that it's properly served. If you wish to present evidence to rebut the Board of Election's

service, you may do so. Okay. The mere fact that you claim you want to find out whether or not the candidate served the papers is, in my view, insufficient to rebut the presumption. If you have evidence that he served it or you wish to go to a Traverse, but to go on a fishing expedition is insufficient to rebut the presumption of the time stamp of the Board, which we normally accept because it is a City office.

MR. SZALKIEWICZ: Yes.

THE COURT: Okay. The in personam jurisdiction

having been established, was there a Board report here?

MR. KITZINGER: Yes, your Honor. There was.

Since it's a citywide office, it would require 3,750 valid signatures. The Board found that the candidate has 89 valid signatures. There are 4,297 submitted, 4,208 of which were determined to be invalid. The vast majority were validated with the subscribing witness, was not enrolled in the Republican party, and this report was adopted unanimously by the Commissioner of Elections.

THE COURT: Could I see the Board report please?

MR. KITZINGER: Of course, your Honor.

THE COURT: Thank you.

(Handing.)

THE COURT: Mr. Sloan, do you have anything to say about the Board report?

MR. SLOAN: Yes. I have a great deal to say

about this.

First place is this whole proceeding starts with a general objection signed by a Mr. Salvatore Caruso. Mr. Salvatore Caruso had three days to file this general objection, he then had another six days to file a specific objection. These specific objections contain completely different allegations than are on the Board report. The specific objections said that there were 4,269 signatures submitted, of which 4,200 were bad signatures, 69 were good signatures. These numbers are just pulled up out of the air. They just invented these numbers. It has no relationship to the truth. It was obvious that Mr. Caruso and Mr. Szalkiewicz never actually looked at the actual signature cards, never looked at the actual objections. They just made up this objection.

I have a copy of the specific objections right here. It's this big bundle of papers. I'd like to hand it up, if possible.

THE COURT: I'll take a look at that. Would you show it to your adversaries first to make sure that they agree that that is a proper copy of the

specification objection?

MR. SLOAN: This is the document Mr. Szalkiewicz served on me, so I assume that that's the document.

THE COURT: So what's your theory to get back on the ballot?

MR. SLOAN: My theory is, number one, the specific objections were utterly fraudulent. They just made blanket statements. All of the signatures except 69 -- I don't know where they got 69, are good and 4,200 were bad. This puts the Board of Elections to the burden of spending a whole weekend hiring temporary workers and other people to come in and check all of these signatures.

And the first thing is every single page --

THE COURT: Mr. Sloan, there is a Board report.

MR. SLOAN: Yeah. I know that, your Honor, but --

THE COURT: They said there is a Board report. The Board report says that you need 3,750 signatures to be found valid, your petition only has 89. Tell me where you're going to reverse the Board's decision to get those signatures back on.

MR. SLOAN: Your Honor, my first point is the Board doesn't get to that until they submit a valid specific objection. If they don't submit a specific

objection, I'm on the ballot.

THE COURT: But did you have an opportunity to oppose that you thought that the specification objections were properly filed before the Board?

MR. SLOAN: Yes, I did. I said the same thing I'm saying here.

THE COURT: And did the Board rule?

MR. SLOAN: Well, what it comes down to in the end is the Board says that the only thing wrong with my petitions –

THE COURT: That's not what I asked you, Counsel – that's not what I asked you, Mr. Sloan.

Did the Board of Elections rule that the specification of objections filed by the respondents were properly served?

MR. SLOAN: I don't think they actually ruled.

THE COURT: They had to, otherwise there wouldn't be a Board report.

MR. SLOAN: I'm not complaining about the service because, in fact --

THE COURT: Well, then they would've ruled that it's sufficient in its merit, otherwise there wouldn't be a Board report.

MR. SLOAN: But the Board report said something different than what the specific objection said.

THE COURT: So what?

MR. SLOAN: Because they should not have been allowed to -- if the specific objections contains false statements, such as none of the subscribing witnesses are registered to vote – see, the specific objections says that none of the subscribing witnesses are objecting to it, all of the subscribing witnesses are; that's why I want you to look at those specific objections and you'll see –

THE COURT: I'm looking it, it says "SW" with "NE", Subscribing Witness Not Enrolled, subscribing witness is not registered.

MR. SLOAN: But, in fact, all of those witnesses are registered to vote. You have 500 sheets of paper saying that all of these subscribing witnesses are not registered to vote. In fact, every one of them are registered to vote. So you have 500, your Honor.

THE COURT: Did you pull the buff cards on each one of these SWs?

MR. SLOAN: Yes, I did.

THE COURT: Do you have certified copies to send to the Court?

MR. SLOAN: No, I don't.

THE COURT: So how are you going to prove your case?

MR. SLOAN: Well, the Board of Elections has the buff cards on all of these people.

THE COURT: Mr. Sloan, you have to go forward to prove your case. I'm asking for an offer of proof on how you intend to prove your case.

MR. SLOAN: Well, I can go to the Board of Elections and print out all of these buff cards of all these subscribing witnesses and show that they were all registered to vote.

THE COURT: Why haven't you already done that?

MR. SLOAN: It never occurred that this question would even come up because I assumed the Board of Elections would tell you that they're all registered to vote because the clerk's reports does not say that they were not registered to vote.

THE COURT: Okay. I will give you a shot.

Counsel, anything in opposition here?

MR. SZALKIEWICZ: Yeah. I'm sorry.

MR. KITZINGER: Your Honor, the vast majority is that they were not enrolled members of the Republican party; that is a requirement of the election law under 6-132(2).

THE COURT: I understand.

Is it your position that these people are not members of the Republican party?

MR. SLOAN: Not the fact that they're not enrolled in the Republican party, but they were registered to vote.

THE COURT: Okay. Well, then that defeats your case.

MR. SLOAN: Wait, wait. I disagree, your Honor, because first, frankly, we didn't even know about this rule. It's not a specifically written rule. I don't think it's there, but Mr. Richman starts --

THE COURT: No, no. Let's stop.

In order for you to be nominated to be the

Republican party nominee for the Office Of Mayor, you have to be nominated by certain people.

MR. SLOAN: Right.

THE COURT: Either members of the Republican party have to fill out the petition; that's in the law; that's required.

MR. KITZINGER: 6-132 subdivision 2, your Honor.

MR. RICHMAN: Your Honor, if we may, so it reads, "there shall be appended at the bottom of each sheet a signed statement of the witness who is a duly-qualified voter of the state and an enrolled voter of the same political party as the voter's qualified to sign the petition."

THE COURT: Very well. Counsel?

MR. SLOAN: No, your Honor. My contention is -- first of all, I didn't know about that. But, secondly, that infringes the constitutional right to vote because it says "only." We're not talking about the people who signed the petition, we're just talking about the witnesses. It says the witnesses have to be Republicans. What is the reason why only Republicans are allowed to witness petitions? Why not Democrats, independents, socialists, greens, yellow people, black people, all kind of different people? It's an unreasonable rule.

There's no valid justification for the rule.
All this rule does is stop the -- enable the Republican party to some interloper, like me for example, who I'm a registered Republican, I want to run for office and give the Republican hierarchy -- the insiders to the power to stop people like me, legitimate Republicans for a very long time, from running for office because they can control the subscribing witnesses because they have access to lots of people who do this kind of work for the Republican party and it's very hard for anybody else to come in and get witnesses. Remember, we're only talking about the witnesses --

THE COURT: Okay. Mr. Sloan, I think I get your point.

Is this the only offer of proof you have, sir?

MR. SLOAN: Well, again, I can get the buff cards –

THE COURT: No. I get your point.

So it's your position that your offer of proof to get you on the ballot is that while you concede that these subscribing witnesses are registered voters, and you also concede they are members of the Republican party –

MR. SLOAN: They're not members.

THE COURT: They're not members of the Republican party, but you believe there is a constitutional violation and I should rule on the constitutional violation to get you on the ballot.

MR. SLOAN: In other words, it infringes upon the constitutional right to petition the government. One, that's not constitutional --

THE COURT: I understand your point. Mr.

Sloan, I understand your point. That argument's been made in at least three federal courts in the past ten years and it hasn't prevailed in any federal jurisdiction in the Second Circuit that I'm aware of.

However, I'll hear you in opposition.

MR. KITZINGER: Your Honor, as to the constitutional statement, the United States Court of

17

Proceedings

Appeals for the Second Circuit ruled in the case of Maslow versus the Board of Elections, at 658 F2d 291 -- I'm sorry, I think it's F3d, 291, 2011. That the specific provision, 6-132 subdivision 2 was valid and constitutionally affirmed. It relied in large measure in the United States Supreme Court case of Lopez V Torres which was handed down a couple of years prior. Also, the plaintiff, as in the Maslow case, sought certiori from the US Supreme Court and that was denied.

In addition, your Honor, there is a procedural problem to the extent that there is a facial challenge to the constitutionality of the provision. Upon information and belief, there's been no notice given to the Attorney General of the State of New York to defend or to provide him notice and an opportunity to defend the constitutionality of this provision.

THE COURT: Mr. Sloan, have you served the Attorney General of the State of New York?

MR. SLOAN: No, I have not, but I have served the Board of Elections which is an agency of the state.

THE COURT: Okay. Very well.

What we're going to do is we are going to wait until eleven o'clock. That will give us a chance to second call to see if Mr. Stevens and Mr. Bozulich appear.

So, gentlemen, take a second.

MR. KITZINGER: Your Honor, there's one last thing I'd like to mention:

In Paragraph 19 of the petition, there's a claim by the candidate, it's verified, "petitioners are new candidates who have never appeared in the ballot before in any election. We have never designated circulating petitions for any party or election previously." In 2004, Mr. Sloan himself sought to be a candidate in what was then the 10th Congressional District. That candidacy was unsuccessfully denied, but there were petitions submitted and there was litigation at minimum for the Eastern District Of New York seeking to validate that petition.

THE COURT: Okay.

MR. SZALKIEWICZ: Also, your Honor, if I may, there's also, in 2010, I believe he ran on the libertarian line for the governor and submitted petitions as well.

Taking it a step further, should you reach the constitutional argument and for what is on Mr. Sloan's favor, what the Court did not rule on are the 1,473 objections to the validity of the signatures that were on those that would determine that the subscribing witnesses are not enrolled. So the bulk of these parties didn't

even sign the petition to begin with and were not

registered as a Republican party.

If we need to go this far, we'd like permission of the Court to either file a verified cross petition, which we have a copy of right here, or would have an answer likewise with an affirmative defense that the invalidating time period should be commenced in order to make sure that these remaining signatures are removed from the petition as well which would bring Mr. Sloan well below the 3,750 signatures he needs in order to be placed on the ballot.

THE COURT: The application that you're asking for, did you submit that as a counterclaim?

MR. SZALKIEWICZ: I did not submit it as a counterclaim, but I can, I have actually followed up in an answer, but I can change it in-between this call and the second call.

THE COURT: But the affirmative defense -- you have filed an affirmative defense to Mr. Sloan's petition?

MR. SZALKIEWICZ: I have it in front of me right now. I was planning on giving it up to the Court.

THE COURT: So you have not served it yet?

MR. SZALKIEWICZ: I have not. It's in front of me.

THE COURT: Because I didn't see it in my file.

MR. SLOAN: Your Honor, may I address the --

THE COURT: No. I hear it. That's all. This is all procedural.

We'll second-call this at, approximately, 11:10. So thank you.

(Case recalled.)

THE COURT: Okay. First of all, it is now 11:10 on August 5th. This matter having been called once for the 9:30 calendar now being second-called at the 11:00 a.m. calendar.

Mr. Stevens, Thomas Stevens, the petitioner, not having appeared and not having appeared pursuant to an attorney or proper representative. A Mr. Richard Bozulich, I'll spell it, B-O-Z-U-L-I-C-H, also a second petitioner not having appeared at the 9:30 call of the calendar, not having appeared at the second call of the calendar at 11:00 a.m., and having no legal or proper representative of same, the application on the order to show cause to validate is hereby dismissed for failure to appear.

In addition, the Court, having herein wishing to correct an error that it earlier made which would apply not only to Mr. Sloan who is here today, but to the other two petitioners, Mr. Bozulich and Mr. Stevens. According

to the affidavit of service, there is an affidavit of service in which a Mr. George Rankoth, spelled R-A-N-K-O-T-H, properly served an order to show cause petition, an affidavit in support on the respondent, Daniel Szalkiewicz, and having also that same person having served an order to show cause affidavit in support on petition on Mr. Salvatore Caruso timely. However, the Board of Elections, according to the information put forward by Mr. Sloan that they were served with a copy of the validating petition, is timed-stamped properly. Also, they were served with a copy of the affidavit in support, but there is no time stamp that shows that Mr. Sloan properly served them with a copy of the order to show cause --

MR. SLOAN: I have the time stamp, your Honor.

THE COURT: Well, let me see it, sir.

(Pause in proceedings.)

MR. SLOAN: Your Honor, the Board of Elections keeps these records and they're not objecting and they don't claim that they weren't served. I don't see why I'm going through all these papers.

(Pause in proceedings.)

MR. SLOAN: I can't find it, but it's definitely at home. I definitely did serve. I definitely do have a time-stamped copy of it.

THE COURT: You have a time stamp of the order to show cause?

MR. SLOAN: The order to show cause, yes, but it's at home.

THE COURT: When did you serve them?

MR. SLOAN: At exactly 4:35. In other words --

MR. KITZINGER: Your Honor, we don't -- the Board doesn't dispute that he received it, but Mr. Sloan's statement that "I served" is somewhat disturbing in light of Mr. Szalkiewicz's prior argument, and --

THE COURT: No. I'll take that as the generic "we." If you believe that he served it, if you believe that "he" meaning means the "we" as the candidates somehow served the order to show cause, I'll take that he has jurisdiction. I just don't have proof that he had served the order to show cause -- the order of the order to show cause.

MR. KITZINGER: But I think he said "I", not "we."

THE COURT: Well, I'm not going to take that as testimony. He's pro se so I'm not going to hold it against him. But you believe that he did serve the order of the order to show cause.

MR. KITZINGER: The Board of Elections received a copy of each of the three documents.

THE COURT: Okay. Thank you, because I only have proof of two.

Very well. Thank you, Mr. Sloan.

Okay. I've heard the application under the offer of proof, and I have the Board report. And under the Board report which says that the number of signatures submitted by Mr. Sloan was 4,297, the total number of invalid signatures was 4,208 - I'm sorry, yeah, 4,208, the total valid was 89 and the number of signatures required was 3,750. Under that application, I've asked for an offer of proof and Mr. Sloan has come forward that he wishes to rely solely on the argument that certain SWs should be reversed by this Court because of the requirement that those SWs be enrolled members of the party.

Under this situation, Mr. Sloan also admits that he was unaware of the requirement that members of the party -- Republican party had to be SWs. In addition to that, he now raises as his sole application a constitutional claim that the requirement under the election law that requires that the SWs on the designating petition be enrolled members of the representative party, however, that application for a constitutional claim is jurisdictionally defective because, under the rules of the court, if you make a

24

Proceedings

constitutional claim in state court, you must serve the Attorney General. And in this particular case, you would've had to serve the Attorney General before the last day to bring the order to show cause to designate a ballot, which was on July 25, 2013.

Having admitted that you haven't served the Attorney General renders the constitutional claim jurisdictionally defective and, therefore, it is denied based on the offer of proof that this is the only claim that you have to reverse the position of the Board that is prima facie defective. It is insufficient proof here to even proceed on an order to show cause -- on the line-by-line order to show cause based on your representations here in court. Therefore, the order to show cause, an application to validate, is hereby denied.

You can order the transcript in which I will so-order the transcript in this period if you wish to proceed and appeal this matter to the First Department. Understand that the First Department will be hearing all appeals on August 12 and August 13, which is next week, so, therefore, ordering the transcript should be expeditious to you.

MR. SLOAN: Yes. I do wish to order the transcript and I will appeal.

THE COURT: Okay. Very well, sir.

Anything else, Counsel?

MR. SLOAN: Yes, your Honor, I would like to address one more issue that we didn't do yet, and that is I'm certain that the signature of Mr. Caruso on the specific objection is a forgery because the signatures are so totally different from the voter registration card. He signed it one way --

THE COURT: Excuse me, sir. I'm not even hearing this application now. I asked for your offer of proof earlier, you didn't even mention this. Now that I've ruled, you want to come up with something new.

MR. SLOAN: No --

THE COURT: No, no. I'm not going to permit you to put that on the record when I asked you what was your offer of proof, sir.

So please, Mr. Sloan, I've ruled. You're obviously an intelligent gentleman. You're reserving your rights for an appeal.

Anything else?

MR. SZALKIEWICZ: Just that a verified answer has been served on the Board and Mr. Sloan -- two others were put in the mail, two other named respondents.

THE COURT: We do have the answer which you handed up today. I point out the answer does not have any counterclaims in it, which would have to be served

26

before July 25th. So it's a general denial.

I do understand that you reserve the right to somehow bring forward other objections, whether that's appropriate or inappropriate at another time, I don't believe so, but the matter has been ruled on. This matter is adjourned.

MR. KITZINGER: Thank you, your Honor.

MR. RICHMAN: Thank you, your Honor.

****

CERTIFIED TO BE A TRUE AND ACCURATE TRANSCRIPT OF THE ORIGINAL STENOGRAPHIC MINUTES TAKEN OF THIS PROCEEDING.

____

VANESSA MILLER
Senior Court Reporter

Made in United States
North Haven, CT
04 November 2026

21772018R00026